THE
MIXOLOGIST
BLUEPRINT

EXPERIENCE NOT REQUIRED

CASEY LINNELL

Copyright © 2025 by Casey Linnell

All rights reserved.

No part of this book may be reproduced or transmitted in any form or by any means, electronic or mechanical, including photocopying, recording, or by any information storage and retrieval system, without written permission from the publisher.

ISBN (hardcover): 979-8-9925962-0-5
ISBN (paperback): 979-8-9925962-2-9

Published in 2025 by Casey's Mixology, LLC

Hudson, WI

www.caseyscocktails.com

Printed in the United States of America

First Edition

Table of Contents

Chapter 1:
Introduction to Flavor & Mixology 1

Chapter 2:
Essential Tools & Techniques. 7

Chapter 3:
The Cocktail Build Process & Dilution Control. 15

Chapter 4:
The Art & Science of Flavor Pairing. 23

Chapter 5:
Cocktail Families & Frameworks. 31

Chapter 6:
Seasonality & Occasion-Based Mixology 39

Chapter 7:
Crafting Signature Cocktails 49

Chapter 8:
Presentation, Garnishing & Experience 57

Chapter 9:
Mastering Advanced Techniques 65

Chapter 10:
Non-Alcoholic & Low-ABV Innovation 73

Chapter 11:
Teaching & Mentorship in Mixology 81

Chapter 12:
The Business of Mixology 89

Appendices 97

Appendix A:
Essential Flavor Pairing
Cheat Sheets 99

Appendix B:
Cocktail Measurement Conversions 101

Appendix C:
Glossary of Mixology Terms 103

Appendix D:
Industry Resources & Further Reading 105

Appendix E:
Classic Cocktail Ratios & Templates 107

Final Thoughts:
The Never-Ending Journey of Mixology 109

CHAPTER 1:
Introduction to Flavor & Mixology

The Language of Taste

EVERY GREAT COCKTAIL STARTS WITH an understanding of flavor—how it moves, how it interacts, and how it lingers on the palate. A well-crafted drink isn't just about throwing together ingredients that sound good. It's about knowing *why* they work together.

At its core, flavor is a multi-sensory experience. Taste, aroma, texture, and even temperature all play a role in how we perceive a drink. The same way a chef layers flavors in a dish, a skilled mixologist constructs a cocktail with balance in mind.

So, let's break it down.

The Three Pillars of Cocktail Balance

A truly great cocktail is about **harmony**—not just between ingredients, but in how the drink interacts with the palate. Every well-made cocktail follows three essential **balance principles**:

1. Balancing Sweet, Sour, and Bitter

The foundation of many cocktails relies on the relationship between **sweet, sour, and bitter** flavors. Each plays a distinct role:

- **Sweetness (Sugar, Syrups, Liqueurs)** – Softens acidity and bitterness, rounding out harsh edges.
- **Sourness (Citrus, Vinegars, Shrubs)** – Cuts through sweetness and provides brightness.
- **Bitterness (Amaro, Bitters, Coffee)** – Adds depth, complexity, and prevents a drink from being cloying.

EXAMPLE: A **Whiskey Sour** works because the **sweetness of simple syrup** balances the **sharp acidity of lemon juice**, while a dash of bitters can add an extra layer of depth.

2. Balancing Alcohol (Strength & Dilution)

Cocktails should never feel too harsh or too weak—**finding the right dilution and alcohol balance is key.**

- **Too strong?** Add dilution (shaking, stirring, or ice control) to soften the heat.
- **Too weak?** Reduce dilution or incorporate stronger modifiers (fortified wines, amaro, or liqueurs).
- **Too overpowering?** Use fats (egg white, coconut, or cream) or sweetness to round out the burn.

EXAMPLE: A **Negroni** (Gin + Campari + Sweet Vermouth) works because **dilution during stirring** allows the **boozy elements to mellow and integrate** without overpowering.

3. Balancing Flavor (Depth & Complexity)

A great cocktail isn't just about strength or sweetness—it's about **creating depth and making the flavors linger.**

- **Use contrasting elements** – If a drink is too one-dimensional, add **spice, umami, or herbal complexity.**
- **Layer ingredients carefully** – Spirits, liqueurs, bitters, and garnishes should **enhance** rather than overpower each other.
- **Play with texture** – Creamy, carbonated, silky, or tannic elements can **affect how a drink feels and how flavors unfold.**

EXAMPLE: A **Mai Tai** isn't just a tropical drink—it balances **rum's depth, almond orgeat's nuttiness, citrus's brightness, and the rich texture from crushed ice.**

Why Some Flavors Just Belong Together

There's a reason certain combinations feel intuitive—strawberries and cream, lemon and honey, coffee and chocolate. The magic lies in molecular compatibility. Ingredients that share key aroma compounds tend to complement each other.

FOR EXAMPLE:

- **Basil & Strawberry:** Both contain eugenol, a compound also found in cloves, making them natural partners.
- **Coconut & Lime:** The creamy sweetness of coconut tempers the sharp acidity of lime, creating balance.

- **Chocolate & Chili:** A combination that dates back to ancient Mesoamerican cultures, where the heat of chili enhances the depth of chocolate's bitterness.

Cocktails follow the same logic. A well-paired drink doesn't just taste good—it feels *right*.

Cultural & Historical Influence on Flavor Pairings

Mixology isn't just science; it's history in a glass. Regional ingredients and culinary traditions have shaped cocktail pairings for centuries.

- **Mexico:** Lime and chili are a staple in everything from margaritas to micheladas. The acidity of lime balances heat, creating a bold and refreshing profile.
- **Japan:** Subtlety and precision define Japanese mixology. Ingredients like yuzu, matcha, and shiso create cocktails that are light yet complex.
- **The American South:** Sweet and bitter pairings dominate, as seen in drinks like the Mint Julep, where sugar tames the boldness of whiskey and mint adds a cooling effect.

Understanding the roots of these pairings allows for deeper creativity. A twist on a classic can respect tradition while bringing something new to the table.

The Role of Texture & Temperature

Flavor isn't just about taste—it's about *feel*. A Negroni on the rocks versus one served up has a completely different impact because dilution and temperature change how flavors interact.

- **Cold drinks mute sweetness:** That's why frozen cocktails often need extra sugar or fruit to taste balanced.
- **Foam creates a luxurious mouthfeel:** Egg white in a Whiskey Sour softens acidity while giving the drink a silky texture.
- **Carbonation brightens flavors:** Think about how a French 75 feels so much lighter with Champagne bubbles carrying the citrus and gin.

Texture is often the missing link in a great cocktail. A well-placed element—whether it's a smooth, clarified milk punch or a bracing, high-acid spritz—can elevate a drink from good to unforgettable.

Looking Ahead

Now that you understand **how cocktails achieve balance**—through sweetness, acidity, bitterness, alcohol strength, and depth of flavor—it's time to focus on the **tools and techniques that bring them to life**. In the next chapter, we'll explore the **essential equipment every mixologist needs**, from shakers and strainers to infusions and carbonation, along with the **fundamental techniques** that ensure precision and consistency in every drink you create.

CHAPTER 2:

Essential Tools & Techniques

A PAINTER NEEDS BRUSHES. A chef needs knives. A mixologist? A well-stocked bar with the right tools and the knowledge to use them. Great cocktails don't happen by accident—technique matters just as much as ingredients. Whether you're stirring a simple Old Fashioned or infusing a fat-washed whiskey, mastering the fundamentals is what separates a good drink from a great one.

Let's start with the essentials.

The Must-Have Bar Tools

You don't need a drawer full of gadgets to make a great cocktail, but a few key tools will elevate your craft:

1. The Shaker

The backbone of any cocktail bar. There are two main types:

- **Boston Shaker:** A two-piece set (metal tin + mixing glass or second tin). Pros love it for its efficiency, but it takes some practice to master the seal.

- **Cobbler Shaker:** Comes with a built-in strainer and lid. Easier for beginners but prone to leaking and also sticking when cold.

USE FOR: Sours, Margaritas, Daiquiris—anything with citrus, egg white, or cream that needs aeration.

2. Mixing Glass

For spirit-forward cocktails that require a gentle touch. A sturdy, weighted glass lets you stir with control, chilling the drink without over-diluting it.

USE FOR: Old Fashioneds, Manhattans, Negronis.

3. Bar Spoon

Not just for stirring! A proper bar spoon allows for precision layering, gentle aeration, and even muddling delicate ingredients.

PRO TIP: The twisted handle helps with controlled stirring—always stir in one direction for a smooth, velvety texture.

4. Strainers

- **Hawthorne Strainer:** The coiled spring catches ice and pulp, perfect for shaken drinks.
- **Fine-Mesh Strainer:** For double-straining shaken cocktails, catching small ice shards or fruit bits.
- **Julep Strainer:** Fits inside a mixing glass for stirred drinks.

Use fine-mesh strainers when you want a smooth, refined texture without excess dilution.

5. Muddler

Essential for releasing oils and juices from fresh ingredients like mint, citrus, or berries. Avoid metal or lacquered wood muddlers—they can impart off-flavors.

USE FOR: Mojitos, Caipirinhas, and Old Fashioned variations.

6. Jiggers

Precision is everything in mixology. Free-pouring may look impressive, but consistency wins every time. A Japanese-style jigger (tall, narrow) is more accurate than a standard double jigger.

USE FOR: Measuring spirits, syrups, and modifiers precisely.

7. Knives & Peelers

Sharp knives make for clean citrus slices, and a good peeler is essential for creating elegant garnishes. A channel knife can carve intricate citrus twists.

PRO TIP: Express citrus peels over your drink before dropping them in—the oils make all the difference.

Mastering Cocktail Techniques

Having the right tools is one thing; knowing how to use them is another.

Shaking vs. Stirring: When to Use Each

The golden rule:

- **Shake** when a drink contains citrus, dairy, or egg white—these ingredients need aeration and emulsification.
- **Stir** when the drink is all spirits—you want a smooth, silky texture, not air bubbles.

How to Shake Properly:

- Add ingredients and then ice to the shaker tin.
- Seal tightly and hold with both hands.
- Shake hard for 10–15 seconds, aiming for a horizontal motion rather than up-and-down.
- Strain immediately to avoid over-dilution.

Want extra texture? Try a dry shake (vigorously shaking **without ice** for 10 to 15 seconds) first when using egg whites, then shake another 10 seconds with ice.

How to Stir Like a Pro:

- Add liquid ingredients and then ice to a mixing glass.
- Stir with a bar spoon, keeping movement smooth and consistent.
- Aim for 15–20 seconds, until the glass feels frosty.
- Strain into a chilled glass.

If the ice is clinking loudly, you're stirring too aggressively. The goal is silent, controlled motion.

Advanced Techniques for Elevating Your Cocktails

1. Fat-Washing: Adding Richness & Depth

Fat-washing infuses spirits with oils from ingredients like butter, coconut, or bacon. The process softens harsh alcohol edges while adding silky texture.

How to Fat-Wash a Spirit:

- Add melted fat (e.g., brown butter) to your spirit.
- Let it sit at room temperature for a few hours.
- Freeze the mixture—fat will solidify on top.
- Strain through a fine-mesh sieve or cheesecloth.

Try a brown butter-washed bourbon for a next-level Old Fashioned.

2. Clarification: Achieving Crystal-Clear Cocktails

Clarification removes solids from a drink while preserving its flavor, resulting in a smooth and visually striking cocktail.

Milk-Washing Method:

- Add milk to an acidic cocktail (like a citrus-based punch).
- Let the milk curdle—it's weird, but trust the process.
- Strain through a coffee filter or fine-mesh sieve.

- The result? A silky-smooth, clear cocktail with a luxurious mouthfeel.

Clarified Piña Coladas taste like magic—pure tropical flavor without the heaviness.

3. Carbonation:
Making Cocktails Lighter & Brighter

Adding bubbles to a cocktail can completely change its character.

- Use a **soda siphon** to carbonate still drinks.
- Try a **forced carbonation method** with a CO2 charger for precise control.

Want to make a sparkling Negroni? Batch it, carbonate it, and serve over ice.

4. Temperature Control & Ice Strategy

Ice isn't just for chilling—it controls dilution and texture.

- **Crushed Ice:** Ideal for tropical drinks (Mai Tai, Swizzle) because it dilutes quickly.
- **Large Ice Cubes:** Perfect for slow-sipping cocktails like Old Fashioneds, reducing dilution.
- **Collins Spears:** Long, thin ice cubes for highballs, keeping drinks cold without watering them down.

PRO TIP: Clear ice melts slower than cloudy ice—clear ice is achieved through directional freezing.

Setting Yourself Up for Success

Now that you understand the essential tools, techniques, and the science of dilution, you're ready to take the next step—**mastering the cocktail build process**. In the next chapter, we'll explore how different cocktail structures influence dilution, balance, and texture, ensuring that every drink you create is perfectly chilled, well-integrated, and expertly crafted.

CHAPTER 3:

The Cocktail Build Process & Dilution Control

A COCKTAIL IS MORE THAN just ingredients—it's a delicate balance of **flavors, temperature, and dilution**. Mastering the **cocktail build process** ensures that drinks are consistent, properly chilled, and perfectly diluted every time.

Dilution is one of the **most overlooked yet crucial elements** in mixology. Too little dilution and a drink tastes harsh and unbalanced. Too much, and it becomes weak and watery. Understanding **how and when to introduce water** is a key skill that separates a good mixologist from a great one.

This chapter will break down the **four essential cocktail builds**, how to control dilution for each, and techniques for precision.

The Role of Dilution in Cocktails

Water is an invisible ingredient in nearly every cocktail. Whether added through shaking or stirring, it:

- Softens harsh alcohol edges
- Balances flavors by integrating ingredients

- Enhances texture & mouthfeel
- Controls temperature for a refreshing or warming experience

---

FACT: The average cocktail has ¾ oz to 1 oz of **water** after proper dilution. That means getting it right is just as important as choosing the right spirit or modifier.

The Four Cocktail Build Methods & Their Dilution Factors

Every cocktail follows one of four primary build processes. Each method requires different **levels of dilution and temperature control**.

1. Stirred Cocktails: Precision & Silkiness

Best for **spirit-forward drinks**
(e.g., Manhattan, Negroni, Old Fashioned).
Goal: Smooth texture, slow dilution, integrated flavors.
Ideal Dilution: 10–15% of the drink's final volume.

How to Stir Properly:

1. In a **mixing glass** add all ingredients then add a generous amount of ice (use large, dense cubes for better control).
2. Insert a **long-handled bar spoon** and stir smoothly **(30-40 revolutions)**—not too fast or aggressive.
3. Strain into a chilled glass, using a julep or Hawthorne strainer.

KEY TIP: If the ice clinks loudly, you're stirring too fast. The goal is to move the ice smoothly without over-diluting the drink.

2. Shaken Cocktails: Aeration & Emulsification

Best for **citrus, dairy, or egg white cocktails**
(e.g., Margarita, Daiquiri, Whiskey Sour).
Goal: Rapid chilling, controlled dilution, and texture creation.
Ideal Dilution: 15–25% of the drink's final volume.

How to Shake Properly:

1. In the large **shaker tin** add all ingredients except for carbonated ingredients (don't want to make a pipe bomb).
2. Fill halfway with ice (**cubed ice is best; crushed ice dilutes too quickly**).
3. Seal the shaker tightly and shake **vigorously for 10-15 seconds**.
4. Strain immediately to avoid over-dilution.

KEY TIP: **Dry Shake for Egg Whites** – If making a drink with egg white (e.g., Whiskey Sour), shake **without ice first** to create a rich, frothy texture.

---

3. Built Cocktails: Minimal Dilution & Control

Best for **highballs, simple spirit-mixer drinks**
(e.g., Gin & Tonic, Dark & Stormy).
Goal: Slow dilution over time, balanced carbonation.
Ideal Dilution: Varies depending on ice-to-liquid ratio.

How to Build a Cocktail in the Glass:

1. Fill the glass **completely with ice** (full cubes work best for controlled dilution).
2. Pour in **spirit first**, then **carbonated mixer last** to preserve bubbles.
3. Gently stir or layer for a balanced mix.

KEY TIP: Never pour carbonated ingredients **before spirits**—it flattens the drink and reduces its brightness.

4. Batched Cocktails: Speed & Efficiency

Best for **pre-mixed cocktails served at events or bars** *(e.g., Negronis, Old Fashioneds).*
Goal: Maintaining consistency and avoiding over-dilution.
Ideal Dilution: Pre-compiled before chilling to match final serving dilution.

How to Batch a Cocktail Correctly:

1. Combine ingredients in large a quantity, keeping the proper ratio, **in advance**.
2. Store in **glass bottles in the fridge** to keep cold.
3. Shake, stir, or pour over ice when ready.

KEY TIP: If serving batched drinks for a friendly event, using the punch bowl can provide ease for guests to serve themselves while still enjoying a quality cocktail.

Mastering Ice for Optimal Dilution

The **type and size of ice** drastically affect a cocktail's dilution rate.

Ice Type	Best For	Dilution Speed
Large Clear Cubes	Old Fashioneds, Negronis	Slow
Standard Cubes	Shaking, Highballs	Medium
Crushed Ice	Juleps, Swizzles, Tropical Drinks	Fast
Collins Spears	Highballs (Gin & Tonic, Mojito)	Medium-Slow
Flavored Ice	Spirit-forward cocktails (infused ice)	Slow (adds flavor)

KEY TIP: Always use **clear ice** (made with directional freezing techniques) for slower dilution and a refined look.

Troubleshooting Dilution Mistakes

Problem: Cocktail is too diluted.

- Use **larger, denser ice** (avoid wet or broken ice).
- Shake/stir for a shorter time.
- Adjust recipe balance to account for excess water.

Problem: Cocktail is too strong.

- Stir/shake longer to incorporate more dilution.
- Serve over ice to allow continued dilution while drinking.
- Add a few drops of water and re-mix.

Problem: Ice melts too fast in a built drink.

- Use larger cubes of ice—less surface area means slower melting.
- Use **Collins spears** in highballs to keep dilution steady.

Final Thoughts: Precision in the Build Process

Controlling dilution is **one of the most overlooked yet essential skills** in mixology. Once mastered, it ensures that **every drink is perfectly crafted, every time.**

Key takeaways:

- Stirred cocktails need slow, controlled dilution.
- Shaken cocktails need rapid aeration & balance.
- Built drinks need proper ice structure & carbonation control.
- Batched cocktails provide speed & efficiency.

Now that you've mastered the **cocktail build process and the science of dilution**, you're ready to explore the next essential skill—**flavor pairing**. In the next chapter, we'll dive into the **art and science of combining ingredients**, learning how to create depth, contrast, and balance in cocktails through complementary and unexpected flavor pairings.

CHAPTER 4:

The Art & Science of Flavor Pairing

A GREAT COCKTAIL ISN'T JUST a mix of ingredients—it's a carefully balanced experience. The best drinks have harmony, contrast, and just enough surprise to keep the palate intrigued. Understanding **why** flavors work together is the key to moving beyond recipes and crafting your own signature cocktails.

This chapter will break down the science and artistry behind pairing flavors, from classic combinations to unexpected duos that create magic in a glass.

How We Perceive Flavor

Before we dive into pairings, let's break down how the brain processes flavor.

- **Taste** (Sweet, Sour, Bitter, Salty, Umami) – Detected by the taste buds.
- **Aroma** – 80% of what we "taste" comes from the nose.
- **Texture & Mouthfeel** – Creaminess, carbonation, viscosity, temperature, and tannins (that drying sensation from wine or tea).

A good cocktail isn't just about taste—it should engage **all three** elements for a complete sensory experience.

The Building Blocks of Flavor Pairing

There are three main ways to combine flavors:

1. Complementary Pairings (Enhancing Similar Flavors)

These are flavors that naturally go together because they share key aroma compounds. They reinforce each other and create a smooth, cohesive profile.

- **Strawberry & Basil** (both contain eugenol, also found in cloves)
- **Vanilla & Oak** (common in aged spirits like bourbon)
- **Coconut & Pineapple** (both have lactones, creating tropical depth)

EXAMPLE COCKTAIL: A Basil-Strawberry Daiquiri enhances the natural fruity sweetness while adding depth with herbal notes.

---

2. Contrasting Pairings (Balancing Opposites)

These pairings work by **creating tension**—where one ingredient softens or sharpens another. This is where balance becomes key.

- **Sweet & Sour** (a classic in almost every cocktail, from Margaritas to Daiquiris)
- **Bitter & Sweet** (Negronis, Espresso Martinis)
- **Fat & Acid** (fat-washed spirits with citrus)

EXAMPLE COCKTAIL: A Honey-Ginger Whiskey Sour—where the spicy heat of ginger contrasts with the smoothness of honey and the brightness of lemon.

3. Unexpected Pairings (Pushing Boundaries)

Some of the most exciting cocktails come from unusual flavor pairings that challenge expectations. These work because of their shared chemical compounds or their ability to create intriguing contrasts.

- **Chocolate & Blue Cheese** (both contain methyl ketones, giving a rich, creamy depth)
- **Black Pepper & Strawberry** (spicy heat brings out the fruit's natural sweetness)
- **Lavender & Lemon** (floral and citrus brightness work in harmony)

EXAMPLE COCKTAIL: A Lavender Lemon Collins—herbal and floral notes balance out the sharp citrus and gin botanicals.

Using the Flavor Wheel for Cocktail Creation

A flavor wheel is an invaluable tool for mixologists. It visually maps out how different flavors relate to each other, helping to inspire new pairings.

How to Use a Flavor Wheel in Mixology

1. Pick a base spirit—gin, whiskey, rum, tequila, etc.
2. Identify its dominant flavors (e.g., gin = botanical, citrus, herbal).

3. Find complementary or contrasting ingredients within the same wheel category.
4. Experiment with texture—carbonation, creaminess, or foam—to enhance balance.

TRY THIS: If you start with **gin**, you might notice it has herbal and floral notes. That could lead you to pair it with **elderflower** or **grapefruit**, then contrast it with **black pepper** for spice. A simple google search for '**cocktail flavor wheel**' will provide multiple options.

Pairing by Season & Mood

Flavors can also be paired based on seasonal ingredients and the emotional experience you want to evoke.

Spring & Summer: Bright & Refreshing

- **Cucumber & Mint** – Light, cooling, and crisp.
- **Melon & Basil** – Fresh, slightly sweet, and herbaceous.
- **Coconut & Lime** – Tropical and citrusy.

EXAMPLE COCKTAIL: A Melon-Basil Spritz—juicy, green, and slightly herbal, perfect for warm weather.

Autumn & Winter: Warm & Spiced

- **Apple & Cinnamon** – Classic cozy pairing.
- **Cranberry & Rosemary** – Tart fruit with herbal complexity.

- **Smoky Scotch & Honey** – Deep, warming, and sweetly rich.

EXAMPLE COCKTAIL: A Smoked Honey Old Fashioned—bourbon, smoked honey, and orange bitters for a cold-weather sipper.

Creating Your Own Signature Pairings

Now that you understand **why** certain flavors work together, let's apply these principles to craft your own cocktail.

Step-by-Step Pairing Exercise:

1. **Choose a Base Spirit:** What are you in the mood for?

    » Rum (Tropical, vanilla, caramel notes)

    » Gin (Herbal, citrusy, floral)

    » Whiskey (Oak, spice, caramel, smoke)

2. **Identify Its Dominant Flavor Notes:**

    » Is it smoky? Fruity? Herbal?

3. **Find a Complementary or Contrasting Ingredient:**

    » Example: Whiskey (caramel, oak) → **Coffee or Chocolate** for depth, **Orange or Lemon** for contrast.

4. **Consider Texture & Temperature:**

    » Would carbonation make it brighter?

    » Would fat-washing add body?

5. **Test & Refine:**
   » Try different ratios.
   » Adjust with acid or sweetness if needed.
   » Use small taste tests to tweak balance.

EXAMPLE:
- Base: **Tequila** (earthy, vegetal)
- Complementary: **Pineapple** (tropical, sweet)
- Contrast: **Jalapeño** (spicy heat)
- Texture: **Shaken with ice, served up with a chili salt rim**

RESULT? **A Spicy Pineapple Margarita with depth and balance.**

The Next Step in Your Flavor Journey

Now that you have a deeper understanding of **why** flavors work together, you're ready to start building cocktails with confidence. In the next chapter, we'll take this knowledge and apply it to **cocktail families and frameworks**, breaking down classic structures and showing you how to experiment within them.

Grab your shaker—it's time to start mixing with purpose.

CHAPTER 5:
Cocktail Families & Frameworks

GREAT COCKTAILS MAY SEEM WILDLY different from one another, but they all follow a handful of fundamental templates. These **cocktail families** act as blueprints, showing how different spirits, modifiers, and techniques come together to create balanced drinks.

Once you understand these core structures, you can start experimenting—swapping ingredients, adjusting proportions, and creating new flavors while maintaining a solid foundation.

In this chapter, we'll break down the major cocktail families, explore their classic forms, and show how to innovate within them.

The Core Cocktail Families

All cocktails fall into a few major categories. Understanding these allows you to recognize patterns and develop new drinks with confidence.

1. The Old Fashioned Family:
Spirit-Forward Simplicity

Formula:
Base spirit + sugar + bitters + water

The **Old Fashioned** is one of the oldest cocktails, dating back to the 1800s. It relies on a simple balance of spirit, sweetness, and bitterness.

Classic Example:
- **Old Fashioned** (Whiskey + Sugar + Bitters)

Variations & Twists:
- **Rum Old Fashioned** (Aged Rum + Demerara Syrup + Angostura Bitters) – A tropical take with caramel and spice notes.
- **Tequila Old Fashioned** (Reposado Tequila + Agave Syrup + Chocolate Bitters) – Earthy, smooth, and slightly smoky.
- **Smoked Maple Old Fashioned** (Bourbon + Maple Syrup + Smoked Orange Bitters) – Rich and warming with smoky depth.

How to Experiment:
- Swap the spirit (rum for whiskey, tequila for gin).
- Adjust the sweetener (honey instead of sugar, maple syrup for depth).
- Change the bitters (chocolate bitters, orange bitters, or even chili tinctures).

2. The Sour Family:
Balance of Sweet & Tart

Formula:
Base spirit + citrus + sweetener

Sours are all about balance—tart acidity from citrus, sweetness from syrups or liqueurs, and the depth of the base spirit.

Classic Example:

- **Whiskey Sour** (Whiskey + Lemon + Simple Syrup)

Variations & Twists:

- **Daiquiri** (Rum + Lime + Simple Syrup) – A tropical take on the sour format.
- **Margarita** (Tequila + Lime + Orange Liqueur) – Uses Cointreau instead of simple syrup for extra complexity.
- **Bee's Knees** (Gin + Lemon + Honey) – Honey adds floral sweetness.

How to Experiment:

- Change the citrus (grapefruit instead of lime, yuzu for brightness).
- Try different sweeteners (agave nectar, ginger syrup, or spiced honey).
- Add an egg white for a velvety texture and creamy mouthfeel.

3. The Highball Family:
Refreshing & Effervescent

Formula:
Base spirit + carbonated mixer

Highballs are light, easy-drinking, and rely on dilution and carbonation to enhance flavor. The key to a great highball is **proper ice and balance**—too much dilution ruins the drink, while too little makes it harsh.

Classic Example:

- **Gin & Tonic** (Gin + Tonic Water + Lime)

Variations & Twists:

- **Moscow Mule** (Vodka + Ginger Beer + Lime) – Spicy and refreshing.
- **Paloma** (Tequila + Grapefruit Soda + Lime) – A citrusy alternative to a Margarita.
- **Whiskey Highball** (Whiskey + Soda Water) – Clean and crisp, showcasing the whiskey.

How to Experiment:

- Swap the soda (green tea soda, coconut water, or hopped sparkling water).
- Infuse the spirit (cucumber-infused gin in a G&T, or vanilla-infused rum in a Cuba Libre).
- Use flavored ice cubes that melt and change the drink's character over time.

4. The Martini & Manhattan Family:
Elegant & Aromatic

Formula:
Base spirit + fortified wine (vermouth) + optional bitters

These cocktails emphasize the **nuances of the spirit**, with subtle sweetness and botanical complexity from vermouth or aromatized wines.

Classic Examples:

- **Martini** (Gin + Dry Vermouth + Lemon Twist or Olive) – Crisp and herbal.
- **Manhattan** (Rye Whiskey + Sweet Vermouth + Bitters) – Rich, complex, and slightly sweet.

Variations & Twists:

- **Vesper Martini** (Gin + Vodka + Lillet Blanc) – Stronger, more floral than a classic Martini.
- **Reverse Manhattan** (More vermouth than whiskey) – Lower ABV and smoother.
- **Coffee Negroni** (Gin + Sweet Vermouth + Cold Brew Coffee + Campari) – Adds depth and an unexpected kick.

How to Experiment:

- Adjust the vermouth ratio (drier or sweeter).
- Use different aromatized wines (Lillet, Cocchi Americano, or Madeira).
- Add a rinse (absinthe, sherry, or peated scotch) to enhance aroma.

5. The Tiki Family: Complex & Layered

Formula:
Multiple spirits + citrus + syrup + spice

Tiki cocktails are known for their **deeply layered flavors, tropical ingredients, and bold presentations**. They often combine multiple rums, fresh juices, and unique syrups.

Classic Examples:

- **Mai Tai** (Rum + Lime + Orgeat + Orange Liqueur) – A perfect balance of nutty, citrusy, and boozy.
- **Zombie** (Multiple Rums + Falernum + Citrus + Spices) – High-proof and deeply complex.

Variations & Twists:

- **Jungle Bird** (Rum + Campari + Pineapple) – Tiki meets bitterness.
- **Painkiller** (Rum + Pineapple + Coconut + Nutmeg) – Creamy and indulgent.

How to Experiment:
- Play with spice elements (cinnamon, clove, star anise).
- Swap syrups (passion fruit, allspice dram, or smoked honey).
- Add unexpected bitters (chocolate, coffee, or grapefruit bitters).

Building a Cocktail from a Framework

Now that you understand the core families, let's create a cocktail from scratch using these templates.

EXAMPLE: Creating a New Sour Cocktail
- **Choose a Base Spirit:** Mezcal (smoky, earthy)
- **Pick a Citrus:** Grapefruit (tart but slightly sweet)
- **Select a Sweetener:** Honey syrup (round, floral)
- **Add a Unique Element:** Smoked salt rim for depth

FINAL COCKTAIL:

The Smoked Paloma

- 2 oz Mezcal
- 1 oz Fresh Grapefruit Juice
- ¾ oz Honey Syrup
- ½ oz Lime Juice
- Smoked Salt Rim

Shake and serve over ice—suddenly, you have a unique but **structurally sound** cocktail that follows the Sour template.

Next Steps: Taking Cocktail Design to the Next Level

Now that you can recognize the core cocktail families and start improvising within them, we'll dive deeper into **seasonal and occasion-based mixology** in the next chapter. Understanding how to adapt drinks for different times of year, moods, and celebrations will take your skills even further.

Grab your jigger, because your mixology creativity is about to expand.

CHAPTER 6:

Seasonality & Occasion-Based Mixology

A GREAT COCKTAIL IS MORE than just a combination of ingredients—it's an experience. The best drinks don't just taste good; they feel right for the moment. A crisp, citrusy highball on a hot summer afternoon, a warm spiced toddy by the fire in winter, a festive punch at a holiday gathering—these aren't just drinks, they're memories in a glass.

Seasonality and occasion-based mixology are about **using the right ingredients, flavors, and presentation to match the time, place, and mood**. This chapter will explore how to craft cocktails that feel perfectly suited for any time of year or special event.

The Power of Seasonal Ingredients

Using **seasonal produce** isn't just a chef's philosophy—it's a mixologist's secret weapon. Fresh, in-season ingredients taste better, provide more vibrant flavors, and make cocktails feel naturally suited to the time of year.

Here's a breakdown of **seasonal flavor profiles** and key ingredients to work with:

Spring: Fresh & Floral

Spring cocktails should feel **light, herbal, and slightly floral,** celebrating the return of bright, fresh flavors after winter.

Flavors & Ingredients:

- Fresh herbs (basil, mint, thyme)
- Floral notes (lavender, elderflower, chamomile)
- Berries (strawberries, raspberries)
- Citrus (grapefruit, lemon, yuzu)
- Botanical spirits (gin, aquavit)

SPRING COCKTAIL EXAMPLE:

Elderflower Collins

- 2 oz Gin
- ¾ oz Fresh Lemon Juice
- ½ oz Elderflower Liqueur
- ½ oz Honey Syrup
- Sparkling Water

Shake everything except sparkling water with ice, strain into a Collins glass, and top with soda. Garnish with a lemon wheel and edible flowers.

Summer: Bright & Tropical

Summer cocktails should be **refreshing, juicy, and sometimes a little spicy,** perfect for hot weather.

Flavors & Ingredients:

- Tropical fruits (pineapple, mango, watermelon)
- Cooling herbs (mint, lemongrass)
- Citrusy brightness (lime, orange, passion fruit)
- Spice & heat (chili, jalapeño, ginger)
- Lighter spirits (rum, tequila, mezcal, pisco)

SUMMER COCKTAIL EXAMPLE:

Spicy Watermelon Margarita

- 2 oz Tequila
- 1 oz Fresh Lime Juice
- 1 oz Watermelon Juice
- ½ oz Agave Syrup
- 1 Slice Jalapeño (muddled)

Shake with ice, strain into a rocks glass over fresh ice, and rim with Tajín for a spicy-salty contrast.

Autumn: Warm & Earthy

Autumn cocktails should be **spiced, cozy, and rich**, with flavors that pair well with crisp air and falling leaves.

Flavors & Ingredients:

- Stone fruits (apple, pear, fig)
- Warming spices (cinnamon, nutmeg, allspice, clove)
- Darker spirits (bourbon, rye, aged rum, cognac)
- Nutty & caramelized elements (maple, toasted pecan, browned butter)

AUTUMN COCKTAIL EXAMPLE:

Smoky Apple Old Fashioned

- 2 oz Bourbon
- ½ oz Apple Cider Syrup (apple cider reduced with cinnamon & sugar)
- 2 dashes Angostura Bitters
- Smoked Applewood Garnish

Stir with ice, strain over a large cube, and garnish with a smoked apple slice.

Winter: Rich & Comforting

Winter cocktails should feel **deep, spiced, and warming**, perfect for cold nights and holiday celebrations.

Flavors & Ingredients:

- Dark fruits (cranberry, pomegranate, black cherry)
- Baking spices (ginger, clove, star anise)
- Creamy & rich textures (eggnog, hot buttered rum, Irish coffee)
- Heavier spirits (scotch, brandy, amaro, port)

WINTER COCKTAIL EXAMPLE:

Spiced Cranberry Manhattan

- 2 oz Rye Whiskey
- ¾ oz Sweet Vermouth
- ½ oz Spiced Cranberry Syrup (cranberries, cinnamon, star anise)
- 2 dashes Orange Bitters

Stir with ice, strain into a coupe, and garnish with an orange twist and sugared cranberries.

Occasion-Based Mixology

Beyond seasonality, cocktails can also be tailored to **specific events and experiences**. Here's how to match drinks to different occasions.

Brunch Cocktails: Light & Daytime-Friendly

Brunch drinks should be **bubbly, citrusy, and easy to sip**, balancing flavors that work with rich breakfast foods.

Great Brunch Cocktails:

- **Classic Mimosa** (Sparkling Wine + Orange Juice)
- **French 75** (Gin + Lemon + Champagne)
- **Bloody Mary** (Vodka + Tomato + Spices)

BRUNCH UPGRADE: Try a **Grapefruit-Rosemary Spritz** for a modern twist on the Mimosa.

Holiday & Festive Cocktails: Cozy & Indulgent

Holidays are the perfect time for **batch cocktails, rich flavors, and warm spices**.

Great Holiday Cocktails:

- **Mulled Wine** (Red Wine + Brandy + Spices)
- **Eggnog** (Cognac + Cream + Nutmeg)

- **Hot Buttered Rum** (Dark Rum + Spiced Butter Mix)

FESTIVE UPGRADE: Make a **Sparkling Pomegranate Punch** with Champagne, pomegranate juice, and winter spices for a crowd-pleasing drink.

Wedding & Elegant Gatherings:
Sophisticated & Timeless

For formal occasions, cocktails should be **refined, balanced, and visually stunning**.

Great Wedding Cocktails:

- **French 75** (Gin + Lemon + Champagne)
- **White Negroni** (Gin + Lillet Blanc + Suze)
- **Basil Gimlet** (Gin + Lime + Basil Syrup)

ELEGANT UPGRADE: Serve a **Rose & Cucumber Collins** for a light, floral signature wedding cocktail.

Cocktail Parties & Entertaining:
Easy & Interactive

For cocktail parties, drinks should be **fun, easy to make in batches, and interactive**.

Great Party Cocktails:

- **Punch Bowls** (Sangria, Rum Punch, Bourbon Smash)
- **DIY Margarita Bar** (Variety of fruits, salts, and tequilas for guests to mix)

- **Negroni on Tap** (Pre-batched and served over ice)

PARTY UPGRADE: Set up a **Whiskey Tasting Station** with different styles and suggested pairings.

How to Design a Seasonal or Occasion-Based Menu

When curating a cocktail menu—whether for a bar, event, or home gathering—consider these key elements:

- **Balance:** Offer a variety of spirits, flavors, and intensities.
- **Seasonality:** Use fresh, in-season ingredients for the best flavor.
- **Presentation:** Adjust glassware and garnishes to match the mood.
- **Efficiency:** Consider which drinks can be pre-batched or made quickly.

Sample Seasonal Menu (Autumn Edition)

- **Signature Cocktail:** Spiced Pear Whiskey Sour
- **Refreshing Option:** Honey-Ginger Highball
- **Spirit-Forward Option:** Maple-Smoked Manhattan
- **Low-ABV Option:** Amaro Spritz
- **Non-Alcoholic:** Mulled Apple Cider with Clove

Next Steps: Crafting Signature Cocktails

Now that you understand how to match drinks to seasons and occasions, the next step is to **create your own signature cocktails**. In the next chapter, we'll break down the creative process—how to develop unique recipes, experiment with flavors, and refine your drinks to perfection.

Your mixology skills are about to go from great to unforgettable.

CHAPTER 7:

Crafting Signature Cocktails

A GREAT MIXOLOGIST DOESN'T JUST memorize recipes—they create new ones. Crafting a **signature cocktail** is more than just mixing ingredients; it's about telling a story through flavor, balance, and presentation. Whether you're making a drink for a menu, a special event, or just for fun, the process follows a structured yet creative approach.

In this chapter, we'll break down how to develop your own cocktail recipes, step by step.

Step 1:
Start with a Concept

Before you even pick up a shaker, ask yourself:

- **What's the inspiration?** (A place, a memory, a mood?)
- **Who is this for?** (A whiskey lover, a non-drinker, an adventurous palate?)
- **What experience do you want to create?** (Refreshing, warming, sophisticated?)

A signature cocktail should have **intention** behind it.

FOR EXAMPLE:

- A smoky mezcal cocktail inspired by a beach bonfire.
- A floral gin drink that feels like a spring garden in bloom.
- A dessert-style rum cocktail that tastes like caramelized bananas.

This **theme or emotion** will guide your ingredient choices.

Step 2: Choose Your Base Spirit

Every cocktail starts with a strong foundation—your **base spirit**. This is the primary flavor and backbone of the drink.

Spirit	Flavor Profile	Best Pairings
Gin	Herbal, botanical	Citrus, floral, bitters
Whiskey	Rich, caramel, spice	Honey, vanilla, coffee
Tequila	Earthy, vegetal	Lime, agave, chili
Rum	Sweet, molasses	Tropical fruits, spices
Vodka	Neutral, clean	Almost anything
Brandy	Fruity, oaky	Cinnamon, apple, fig

EXAMPLE: If you're creating a **warming, autumn-inspired drink**, bourbon or aged rum would be a great choice. If you want something **light and refreshing**, gin or tequila might be better.

Step 3: Balance the Flavor Profile

A well-balanced cocktail follows the **Flavor Triangle**:

Strong (Base Spirit) – The backbone of the drink.
Sweet (Modifier) – Syrups, liqueurs, fruit juices.
Sour/Bitter (Counterbalance) – Citrus, vinegar, bitters.

Some classic **balance formulas**:

- **Spirit + Citrus + Sweetener = Sour Cocktail** (e.g., Daiquiri)
- **Spirit + Bitter + Sweet = Aperitif Cocktail** (e.g., Negroni)
- **Spirit + Sugar + Water + Bitters = Classic Cocktail** (e.g., Old Fashioned)

EXAMPLE 1: Creating a new Sour-style cocktail
- Base: **Mezcal** (smoky, earthy)
- Sweet: **Pineapple Juice** (tropical, sweet)
- Sour: **Lime Juice** (acidic balance)
- Unique Twist: **Jalapeño-infused honey** (spice + complexity)

RESULT? **A Smoky Pineapple Mezcal Sour**—bright, smoky, spicy, and balanced.

Step 4: Build Complexity with Modifiers

Modifiers are the **small ingredients that add layers of depth**. These can include:

- **Bitters** (Angostura, orange, chocolate)
- **Liqueurs** (Aperol, Chartreuse, coffee liqueur)
- **Syrups** (honey, cinnamon, ginger, or infused syrups)
- **Tinctures & Extracts** (vanilla, absinthe, saline solution)

EXAMPLE:

- A **lavender-infused syrup** in a Gin Sour adds floral depth.
- A **chocolate bitters dash** in an Old Fashioned enhances the caramel notes.
- A **coffee liqueur float** in a Rum Punch adds richness.

TIP: Start with small amounts (¼ oz or a few dashes) and taste as you go.

Step 5: Consider Texture & Temperature

A great cocktail isn't just about taste—it's also about how it **feels** in your mouth.

Techniques to Adjust Texture:

- **Egg White or Aquafaba** → Adds silkiness *(e.g., Whiskey Sour).*
- **Carbonation** → Adds lightness and brightness *(e.g., French 75).*
- **Crushed Ice** → Creates a fast-melting, refreshing effect *(e.g., Mai Tai).*
- **Fat-Washing** → Adds creaminess and depth *(e.g., Brown Butter Bourbon Old Fashioned).*

EXAMPLE: If you're making a **dessert cocktail**, adding heavy cream or a coconut-washed rum can make it velvety and indulgent.

Step 6: Perfecting the Presentation

People drink with their **eyes first**. A visually stunning cocktail makes an impression before the first sip.

Glassware Selection:

- **Tall & Refreshing?** Use a highball.
- **Short & Spirit-Forward?** Use a rocks glass.
- **Elegant & Sophisticated?** Use a coupe.

Garnishes That Add to Flavor:

- **Citrus Peel** – Express the oils over the drink for aroma.
- **Fresh Herbs** – Smack mint or basil leaves to release their scent.

- **Flavored Sugar or Salt Rims** – Adds an extra layer of taste (e.g., Tajín rim for a Margarita).
- **Edible Flowers & Dehydrated Fruit** – Beautiful and fragrant.

EXAMPLE: A **rosemary-smoked glass** for a bourbon cocktail adds an aromatic experience.

Step 7: Refining & Naming Your Cocktail

Even after you think you've created the perfect drink, **taste and adjust**:

- Too sweet? Add more citrus or bitters.
- Too sour? Increase the sweetener slightly.
- Too boozy? Shake with more ice for dilution.

Once perfected, give it a **memorable name** that reflects the theme or inspiration.

EXAMPLES:
- "Midnight Smoke" (A mezcal-based Negroni twist with coffee notes)
- "Summer in Kyoto" (A yuzu-infused gin spritz)
- "Velvet Reverie" (A creamy Cognac and vanilla dessert cocktail)

A great cocktail name should evoke imagery, emotion, or a sense of place.

Putting It All Together: A Signature Cocktail Case Study

The Honeyed Ember

A rich, smoky, and slightly spiced cocktail inspired by autumn bonfires.

- **Base Spirit:** 2 oz Bourbon
- **Sweet Element:** ¾ oz Honey-Cinnamon Syrup
- **Acid/Bitter Element:** ½ oz Lemon Juice + 2 dashes Chocolate Bitters
- **Unique Element:** Smoked Rosemary Garnish

Instructions: Shake bourbon, honey syrup, lemon juice, and bitters with ice. Strain into a rocks glass over a large cube. Garnish with a smoked rosemary sprig.

Why it works:

- Bourbon's caramel notes pair beautifully with honey.
- Lemon cuts through sweetness for balance.
- Smoked rosemary adds an aromatic layer.

Your Turn: Create Your Own Signature Cocktail

Now, follow the **7-step framework** and craft your own original drink. Experiment, tweak, and **trust your palate**.

In the next chapter, we'll explore **presentation & multi-sensory mixology**, going beyond just flavor to create unforgettable drinking experiences.

The glass is yours—start mixing.

CHAPTER 8:

Presentation, Garnishing & Experience

A COCKTAIL ISN'T JUST ABOUT taste—it's an experience. The best drinks engage **all five senses**, making them more memorable and immersive. The right glassware, garnishes, aromas, textures, and even sound can turn a simple drink into something extraordinary.

This chapter explores **how to elevate cocktail presentation**, create multi-sensory experiences, and make drinks that are as beautiful as they are delicious.

The Psychology of Presentation: Why It Matters

Before the first sip, a cocktail is judged by its **appearance, aroma, and feel**. These elements set expectations and influence perception.

- A well-garnished drink feels premium.
- A mist of citrus oil enhances brightness before the first taste.
- A chilled glass signals a refreshing experience.

The way a drink is served **changes the way it's perceived**—even when the ingredients stay the same.

Glassware: More Than Just Aesthetics

Glassware affects **temperature, aroma, and mouthfeel**. Choosing the right glass enhances the drinking experience.

Choosing the Right Glass for the Right Cocktail

Glass Type	Best For	Why It Works
Coupe	Martinis, Daiquiris	Elegant, wide surface enhances aroma
Highball	Collins, Mojitos	Tall & narrow keeps carbonation fresh
Rocks (Old Fashioned)	Negronis, Old Fashioneds	Sturdy, allows for slow-melting ice
Nick & Nora	Spirit-forward cocktails	Similar to a coupe, but prevents spills
Tiki Mugs	Tropical drinks	Insulated to keep drinks colder longer
Wine Glass	Spritzes, Sangria	Captures aromas and aerates the drink

PRESENTATION TIP: **Chill glassware in advance** for cold cocktails, and warm mugs for hot drinks.

Garnishing Like a Pro

A great garnish is more than just decoration—it should add **flavor, aroma, and interaction.**

Types of Garnishes & When to Use Them

- **Citrus Twists & Peels** – Express oils over the drink to enhance aroma.
- **Herbs** (Mint, Basil, Rosemary) – Smack the herbs before adding to release scent.
- **Salt & Sugar Rims** – Adds texture and contrast to each sip.
- **Edible Flowers** – Beautiful and fragrant (e.g., violets, chamomile).
- **Dehydrated Fruit** – Long-lasting garnish with concentrated flavor.
- **Infused Ice Cubes** – Freeze herbs, fruit, or edible glitter inside for a slow-release effect.

PRO TIP: **Smoke or torch garnishes** (rosemary, cinnamon, or orange peels) to add aroma and spectacle.

Aroma: The Secret Ingredient

80% of what we "taste" is actually **smell**. A drink's aroma can enhance, contrast, or completely transform the flavor experience.

Techniques to Enhance Aroma

- Smoking Glasses & Garnishes:
  - Smoke a glass with a burning cinnamon stick or rosemary sprig.
  - Use a cloche to trap smoke before serving.
- Expressed Citrus Oils:
  - Twist a lemon or orange peel over a cocktail to release its fragrant oils.
- Herbal Sprays & Mists:

> » A spritz of absinthe, rosewater, or lavender tincture adds complexity.

EXAMPLE: A smoked glass for an Old Fashioned enhances its deep, oaky flavors.

Texture: Engaging Mouthfeel in Cocktails

A drink's texture can make it feel **light and effervescent** or **rich and velvety**.

Ways to Manipulate Texture:

- Egg Whites (Foam & Creaminess):
  - » Used in sours (e.g., Whiskey Sour, Pisco Sour) to create a luxurious mouthfeel.
  - » **Alternative:** Use **aquafaba** for a vegan option.
- Carbonation (Light & Refreshing):
  - » Soda water, Champagne, or carbonated cocktails like the French 75 create lift.
- Fat-Washing (Smooth & Silky):
  - » Washing spirits with butter, coconut oil, or brown butter adds richness.

EXAMPLE: Brown Butter Bourbon Manhattan.

- Crushed vs. Clear Ice (Dilution Control):
  » **Crushed ice** speeds up dilution (great for tropical drinks).
  » **Large clear cubes** melt slower (ideal for spirit-forward drinks).

TIP: Freeze **flavored ice cubes** (coffee for an Espresso Martini, fruit juice for a Negroni) to enhance the drink as they melt.

Sound & Interaction: The Final Touch

Cocktails should be interactive—whether through sound, movement, or engagement.

- **Crackling Ice & Fizzing Carbonation** – The pop of a Champagne bottle or the effervescence of a spritz makes a drink more exciting.
- **Interactive Presentation** – Consider drinks that change over time:
  » **Color-Changing Cocktails** (Butterfly Pea Tea shifts from blue to purple with acidity).
  » **Layered Drinks** (Slowly blending elements create a visual experience).
- **Signature Glassware & Themed Servings** – Serving in unique vessels (e.g., skull glasses for a Halloween cocktail) makes drinks more memorable.

EXAMPLE: A tea-smoked glass for a gin cocktail, served under a dome, releasing the aromatic cloud when lifted.

Case Study: Crafting a Multi-Sensory Cocktail

The "Midnight Fog"

A deep, smoky, and aromatic cocktail designed to engage multiple senses.

- **Base Spirit:** 2 oz Mezcal (earthy, smoky)
- **Sweet Element:** ½ oz Honey-Ginger Syrup (warming)
- **Bitter Element:** 2 dashes Chocolate Bitters
- **Aroma:** Smoked Rosemary Mist
- **Texture:** Egg White (for a velvety foam)

Presentation: Served in a chilled coupe under a smoke-filled cloche.

How It Works:

- The rosemary smoke adds aroma before the first sip.
- The velvety foam provides texture contrast.
- The honey-ginger syrup adds depth and warmth.
- The theatrical smoke dome creates a **memorable visual effect**.

Designing a Show-Stopping Signature Cocktail

When creating your own **visually stunning, multi-sensory cocktail**, ask:

- **How does it look?** (Color, clarity, garnishes)
- **How does it smell?** (Aromatics, expressed citrus, smoke)
- **How does it feel?** (Texture, temperature, carbonation)
- **How does it sound?** (Fizz, crackling ice, interactive elements)

- **How does it change?** (Does the drink evolve as you sip?)

A cocktail that engages multiple senses is a cocktail people remember.

Next Steps: Elevating Cocktails with Advanced Techniques

Now that you've mastered **presentation and multi-sensory mixology**, it's time to explore **advanced cocktail techniques**. In the next chapter, we'll dive into **layering flavors, molecular mixology, and sustainable bartending**—pushing the boundaries of what's possible behind your bar.

Your cocktails are about to become unforgettable.

CHAPTER 9:
Mastering Advanced Techniques

A GREAT MIXOLOGIST DOESN'T JUST follow recipes—they push boundaries, experiment, and refine their craft. Advanced techniques in mixology open the door to **new textures, intensified flavors, and cutting-edge presentations**. Whether you want to create layered cocktails, use molecular mixology tricks, or embrace sustainability, this chapter will show you how to elevate your drinks to the next level.

Layering Flavors: The Art of Depth & Complexity

The best cocktails don't just mix flavors; they **layer** them to create depth and intrigue.

Techniques for Layering Flavors:

- **Bitters & Tinctures** – Small but mighty, bitters add complexity and structure.

EXAMPLE: A dash of chocolate bitters in an Old Fashioned adds richness.

- **Float & Layering Liquids** – Different spirits and liqueurs have **varying densities**, allowing for a layered effect.

EXAMPLE: A Pousse-Café cocktail layers colorful liqueurs in a stunning gradient.

- **Infusions & Fat-Washing** – Spirits infused with herbs, spices, or fats gain **new dimensions of flavor**.

EXAMPLE: Coconut fat-washed rum adds tropical richness to a Piña Colada variation.

- **Aromatics First, Flavor Second** – Introduce **smoke, citrus zest, or herbs** before sipping to **prime the palate**.

EXAMPLE: Expressing an orange peel over a Negroni before serving enhances its citrus notes.

Molecular Mixology: Science Meets Art

Molecular techniques take cocktails to the realm of **unexpected textures and dramatic presentation**.

1. Spherification:
Turning Liquids into Caviar-Like Beads

Spherification creates **small, burst-in-your-mouth pearls of liquid**.

- Uses **sodium alginate + calcium chloride** to form a gel around the liquid.

- Common in high-end bars for adding **cocktail caviar** to drinks.

EXAMPLE: Margarita pearls floating in a Tequila Sunrise.

2. Clarification:
Making Crystal-Clear Cocktails

Clarification removes **cloudiness and solids** from citrus or dairy-based drinks, resulting in a **smooth and refined texture**.

Milk-Washing (Clarifying with Dairy)

- When **milk and citrus** mix, the milk curdles, trapping unwanted solids.
- The result is a **clear, silky-textured cocktail** with a rich mouthfeel.

EXAMPLE: A clarified Piña Colada tastes tropical but looks crystal clear.

3. Foams & Airs:
Creating Light, Fluffy Textures

Cocktail foams **add texture and intensity** to drinks without diluting them.

- **Egg White Foam** – Classic technique (e.g., Whiskey Sour).
- **Soy Lecithin Foam** – A **vegan** alternative using an emulsifier.
- **Espuma (Culinary Foam)** – Made with a whipped cream charger for **dense, flavorful foam**.

EXAMPLE: A Salted Honey Foam topping a Smoked Old Fashioned.

4. Smoke & Vapor:
Enhancing Aroma & Drama

Using smoke or vapor adds **a dramatic element and deepens the drink's sensory appeal**.

- **Smoke Rinsing Glasses** – Trap smoke inside before serving.
- **Dry Ice & Liquid Nitrogen** – Creates fog effects (handle with care).
- **Aroma Vapors** – Infuse a drink with scent using essential oils or vapor.

EXAMPLE: A rosemary-smoked glass for a Mezcal Negroni enhances its earthy depth.

Sustainability in Mixology: Reducing Waste & Maximizing Flavor

The modern cocktail movement is embracing sustainability—**reducing waste, upcycling ingredients, and making eco-friendly choices**.

Ways to Make Cocktails More Sustainable:

- **Upcycling Ingredients** – Citrus peels, spent coffee grounds, and herb stems can be repurposed into syrups, garnishes, or infusions.

EXAMPLE: Use leftover pineapple cores to make a **fermented tepache syrup**.

- **Reducing Single-Use Plastics** – Swap plastic straws for metal, glass, or biodegradable alternatives.
- **Using Local & Seasonal Ingredients** – Reduces carbon footprint and enhances freshness.

- **Composting Organic Waste** – Turn citrus husks, herb scraps, and fruit waste into compost for gardens.

Case Study: The Ultimate Advanced Cocktail

The "Golden Eclipse"
(A Multi-Sensory Experience)

A cocktail that combines molecular mixology, layering, and sustainability.

- **Base Spirit:** Fat-washed bourbon (butter-infused for richness)
- **Clarified Ingredient:** Citrus-milk clarified orange juice
- **Molecular Twist:** Coffee liqueur spheres (using reverse spherification)
- **Aroma:** Smoked cinnamon stick garnish

Presentation: Served in a chilled Nick & Nora glass with a gold-dusted rim

Why It Works

- **Layered experience** – Deep bourbon notes, smooth citrus balance, and textural contrast.
- **Multi-sensory elements** – Smoke, gold shimmer, and burst-in-your-mouth coffee pearls.
- **Sustainability** – Uses leftover coffee and clarified citrus to minimize waste.

How to Experiment & Push Boundaries

Want to create your own **advanced signature cocktail**?

Here's how:

1. **Start with a Classic Formula** – Choose a familiar cocktail as a base.
2. **Introduce a Molecular Technique** – Add a clarified element, foam, or sphere.
3. **Use a Unique Presentation Trick** – Smoke, interactive ice, or dramatic glassware.
4. **Balance Science with Simplicity** – Make sure the final drink is **delicious and approachable**.

EXAMPLE: Instead of a classic Mojito, try a **Clarified Mojito Highball with Cucumber Air Foam**.

Next Steps: Non-Alcoholic & Low-ABV Cocktails

As the world of mixology evolves, **low-ABV and non-alcoholic cocktails** are becoming just as innovative and complex as their boozy counterparts. In the next chapter, we'll explore how to craft flavorful, sophisticated zero-proof cocktails that hold their own against any classic drink.

Time to elevate your craft—your most impressive cocktail creations are still ahead.

CHAPTER 10:

Non-Alcoholic & Low-ABV Innovation

Cocktails aren't just about alcohol—they're about **flavor, balance, and experience**. With the rise of mindful drinking, non-alcoholic (zero-proof) and low-ABV cocktails are becoming more sophisticated, offering **depth, complexity, and satisfaction** without the booze.

This chapter will explore how to craft **flavorful, balanced, and exciting non-alcoholic and low-proof drinks**, so whether you're catering to non-drinkers, offering lighter options, or experimenting with new ingredients, you'll have the skills to make memorable no- and low-ABV cocktails.

The Philosophy Behind Non-Alcoholic & Low-ABV Cocktails

A great alcohol-free cocktail should be **as complex and satisfying** as a classic cocktail. This means:

- **Balance:** Just like a traditional cocktail, non-alcoholic drinks need a balance of **sweet, sour, bitter, and aromatic elements**.

- **Mouthfeel:** Alcohol contributes body and texture—so we need to replace that with ingredients like **tannins, spice, or fat-washing.**
- **Depth & Length:** Alcohol has a lingering finish, so we use **bitters, fermented ingredients, and layering** to create a similar effect.

A great non-alcoholic cocktail should never just be juice—it should be a thoughtfully constructed experience.

Understanding Zero-Proof & Low-ABV Ingredients

Since we're removing or reducing alcohol, we need **flavor-packed alternatives** that add complexity.

1. Spirit Alternatives (For Structure & Depth)

Zero-proof spirits mimic the characteristics of traditional spirits using **botanicals, spices, and distillation techniques**.

- **Non-Alcoholic Gin Replacements** – Seedlip Garden 108, Pentire Adrift
- **Non-Alcoholic Whiskey Replacements** – Lyre's American Malt, Ritual Zero Proof Whiskey
- **Non-Alcoholic Aperitifs & Amari** – Wilfred's (bitter orange & rosemary), Ghia (herbal, citrusy)

Want a smoky depth? Try a dash of lapsang souchong tea or charred wood tincture.

2. Bitters & Fermented Ingredients (For Complexity)

Alcohol-free cocktails often lack the **long finish** that spirits provide. To compensate, we add **bitter, tannic, and umami elements.**

- **Non-Alcoholic Bitters** – All the depth, none of the ABV. Look for brands like All the Bitter.
- **Shrubs & Drinking Vinegars** – Acidity and depth, made from **vinegar, fruit, and sugar.**
- **Kombucha & Fermented Teas** – Adds natural effervescence and a tangy bite.
- **Tonic & Herbal Infusions** – Gentian root, quinine, or chamomile can mimic traditional bitters.

EXAMPLE: A non-alcoholic Negroni can be made with Ghia (bitter base), non-alcoholic vermouth, and an orange peel.

---

3. Texture & Mouthfeel Enhancers

Since alcohol contributes body and heat, we replace it with **rich textures and sensory contrast.**

- **Carbonation:** Sparkling water, tonic, or nitrogen-infused cold brew for lightness.
- **Fat-Washing:** Coconut oil, olive oil, or nut butters add smoothness.
- **Aquafaba & Egg White:** For foamy, velvety texture.
- **Tea & Tannins:** Adds dryness and astringency, mimicking spirits.

A tea-infused non-alcoholic Old Fashioned with lapsang souchong can replicate the smokiness of whiskey.

Building a Balanced Zero-Proof Cocktail

A **non-alcoholic cocktail** follows the same structural balance as a classic cocktail:

Base (Structure): Spirit alternative, tea, or strong-flavored liquid.
Acid (Brightness): Citrus, shrubs, or vinegars.
Sweet (Body & Balance): Honey, syrups, or juice.
Bitter & Aromatic (Complexity): Bitters, herbs, tea, or spice.

EXAMPLE: For a **non-alcoholic Whiskey Sour**, use **black tea for depth, lemon for acidity, honey for sweetness, and non-alcoholic bitters for complexity.**

Classic Cocktails, Reimagined Without Alcohol

Let's break down how to create zero-proof versions of classic cocktails without losing depth.

Non-Alcoholic Negroni

- **Base:** 1 oz Wilfred's (bitter orange aperitif)
- **Acid:** 1 oz Non-Alcoholic Sweet Vermouth Alternative
- **Bitterness:** 1 oz Non-Alcoholic Gin or Chamomile Tea
- **Aromatic:** Expressed orange peel

Why it works:

The **bitter aperitif, tannic tea, and citrus oils** provide the same layered complexity as a classic Negroni.

Zero-Proof Espresso Martini

- **Base:** 2 oz Cold Brew Concentrate
- **Sweet:** ½ oz Vanilla Syrup
- **Bitterness:** ½ oz Chicory Root or Non-Alcoholic Amaro
- **Texture:** Aquafaba for froth

Why it works:

The cold brew provides **deep coffee flavors**, while chicory adds **roasted bitterness** to replace vodka's bite.

Low-ABV Spritz Alternative

- **Base:** 2 oz Non-Alcoholic Aperitif (Ghia, Wilfred's)
- **Fizz:** 3 oz Sparkling Water or Kombucha
- **Aromatic:** Orange Slice + Fresh Thyme

Why it works:

A spritz **doesn't need a strong alcohol base**—bubbles, herbs, and bitters create the perfect light sipper.

Designing Your Own Non-Alcoholic Signature Cocktail

Want to create your own **zero-proof or low-ABV masterpiece**? Follow this framework:

1. **Choose a Base:** A strong, structured ingredient (tea, kombucha, non-alcoholic spirit).
2. **Add Brightness:** Citrus juice, shrubs, or vinegar.
3. **Balance Sweetness:** A touch of honey, syrup, or fruit juice.
4. **Introduce Depth:** Bitters, fermented ingredients, or spices.
5. **Adjust Texture:** Carbonation, foam, or infusion techniques.
6. **Finish with Aroma:** Expressed citrus, herbs, or smoke.

EXAMPLE:

- **Base:** Green Tea
- **Brightness:** Yuzu Juice
- **Sweetness:** Jasmine Honey Syrup
- **Depth:** Non-Alcoholic Amaro
- **Texture:** Carbonated
- **Aroma:** Lemon Peel & Torched Rosemary

FINAL DRINK: **"Jasmine Sunrise"** – A refreshing, tea-based cocktail with layered floral complexity.

Final Thoughts & Next Steps

Non-alcoholic and low-ABV cocktails aren't just for people avoiding alcohol—they're for **anyone who loves flavor, balance, and creativity**. With the right techniques, these drinks can be just as satisfying and complex as their full-proof counterparts.

In the next chapter, we'll explore the **art of teaching and mentorship in mixology**, helping you communicate your knowledge, lead tastings, and inspire others to master the craft.

Your journey in mixology is only getting better.

CHAPTER 11:
Teaching & Mentorship in Mixology

MASTERING MIXOLOGY IS AN INCREDIBLE skill—but sharing that knowledge with others is what truly elevates the craft. Whether you're training new bartenders, leading cocktail workshops, or simply introducing friends to the art of cocktails, effective teaching is just as important as technical skill.

In this chapter, we'll break down how to **teach mixology in a way that is engaging, structured, and impactful**. From designing workshops to coaching one-on-one, you'll learn how to pass on your expertise in a way that inspires others.

Why Teaching Mixology Matters

Mixology isn't just about making great drinks—it's about **creating experiences, preserving traditions, and pushing innovation forward**. Teaching allows you to:

- **Improve your own understanding** – Explaining concepts forces you to refine your knowledge.
- **Build a community** – Whether at a bar or in a class, sharing knowledge connects people.

- **Elevate the industry** – Well-trained bartenders mean better cocktails everywhere.
- **Enhance guest experience** – Teaching customers about flavors, pairings, and techniques creates a deeper appreciation for cocktails.

"You don't truly understand something until you can teach it."

Principles of Great Mixology Education

A great teacher doesn't just list facts—they guide students through **hands-on learning, storytelling, and structured skill-building**.

1. Start with the Why

People learn better when they understand the **reason** behind what they're doing. Before teaching a technique, explain:

- Why is this method used?
- What happens chemically when ingredients are mixed?
- How does this affect the final drink?

EXAMPLE: Instead of just saying, "Shake a Whiskey Sour," explain that shaking aerates the drink, emulsifies egg whites, and changes texture.

2. Build Knowledge in Layers

When training a new bartender or student, **structure the learning in progressive steps:**

Beginner Level: Foundation & Balance

- The five tastes & how they interact.
- Basic cocktail structures (Sour, Old Fashioned, Highball).
- How to shake, stir, and strain properly.
- Introduction to spirits and modifiers.

EXERCISE: Have students mix sugar, lemon, and water to learn balance before adding spirits.

Intermediate Level: Technique & Creativity

- Advanced techniques (fat-washing, infusion, carbonation).
- Understanding dilution & ice control.
- Experimenting with unique ingredients & flavor pairings.
- Working efficiently behind a bar.

EXERCISE: Give students a classic cocktail and have them create a twist by changing one element.

Advanced Level: Signature Cocktails & Experience Design

- Developing unique recipes from scratch.
- Advanced garnish & presentation techniques.
- Multi-sensory mixology (aromas, textures, storytelling).
- The psychology of hospitality & guest interaction.

EXERCISE: Have students create a menu of 3 signature drinks with a theme and explain the choices.

3. Engage All Senses in Teaching

People retain information better when they engage **multiple senses** in learning.

- **Visual** – Demonstrate techniques in slow, clear motions. Use diagrams & flavor wheels.
- **Auditory** – Talk through the process. Explain WHY something is happening.
- **Kinesthetic (Hands-On)** – Let students make drinks, adjust flavors, and correct mistakes.
- **Olfactory (Smell)** – Have students compare fresh vs. dried herbs, aged vs. unaged spirits.
- **Taste** – Encourage side-by-side tastings to understand ingredient differences.

EXAMPLE: Have students taste a cocktail before and after adding bitters to see how the flavor evolves.

Training Bartenders: Practical Skills for a Bar Team

If you're leading a team in a bar setting, your approach should focus on **efficiency, consistency, and hospitality**.

Key Areas of Training for Bartenders:

- **Speed & Efficiency** – Teach streamlined movements to reduce wasted time behind the bar.

- **Consistency in Cocktails** – Standardized measurements, proper shaking/stirring times, and accurate pouring.
- **Guest Interaction & Storytelling** – Teaching bartenders how to describe a drink's history and engage guests.
- **Troubleshooting & Adaptation** – What to do if a drink is too sweet, too sour, or if a customer requests modifications.

EXERCISE: Run a speed test where bartenders must make three drinks in two minutes while maintaining quality.

Teaching Cocktail Classes & Workshops

Cocktail workshops are a great way to engage enthusiasts, train professionals, or elevate a bar's offerings.

How to Structure a Great Cocktail Class:

1. **Set the Theme & Goal** – Example: "Classic Cocktails 101" or "Holiday Cocktails & Garnishes."
2. **Start with the Basics** – Explain balance, structure, and technique before jumping into recipes.
3. **Demonstrate Each Drink Clearly** – Show one cocktail at a time, explaining each step.
4. **Let Participants Make Their Own** – Hands-on mixing is key to retention.
5. **Encourage Experimentation** – Offer optional modifiers so attendees can tweak their drinks.
6. **Wrap Up with Q&A & Takeaways** – Provide a recipe sheet so participants can practice at home.

PRO TIP: Always have pre-measured ingredients for efficiency, and prep garnishes in advance to keep things smooth.

How to Explain Flavor Theory to Guests

One of the most valuable skills a bartender or educator can have is **describing flavors in a way that excites and informs guests**.

- **Use Familiar Comparisons** – Instead of saying a whiskey is "high in esters," describe it as "like caramelized banana."
- **Tell a Story** – Instead of just listing ingredients, explain why they work together.
- **Use Sensory Cues** – Ask guests to smell an ingredient first before tasting to connect aroma with flavor.
- **Encourage Exploration** – Suggest flavor modifications to suit personal taste preferences.

EXAMPLE: Instead of saying, *"This cocktail is citrus-forward,"* try: *"This cocktail has a bright lemon backbone, balanced by the warmth of honey and a whisper of herbal depth from thyme."*

The Future of Mixology Education

As the cocktail world evolves, **so does the way we teach it**. Future mixology education will incorporate:

- **Virtual & Online Cocktail Classes** – Expanding access to professional-level training.

- **Sustainability-Focused Training** – Teaching bars to reduce waste and use eco-friendly practices.
- **Flavor Science & Sensory Education** – More focus on the chemistry of taste perception.
- **Interactive Cocktail Menus & Tableside Experiences** – Bringing education directly to the guest experience.

The best bartenders aren't just mixing drinks—they're educators, storytellers, and innovators.

Next Steps: The Business of Mixology

Teaching mixology is an art—but **turning it into a business is a whole different challenge**. In the next chapter, we'll explore the **business side of mixology**, from menu design and pricing strategies to branding and career development.

Your knowledge is growing—soon, you'll be turning your craft into something even bigger.

CHAPTER 12:

The Business of Mixology

Mixology isn't just about crafting great drinks—it's also about **understanding the business behind the bar**. Whether you're managing a cocktail program, opening your own bar, or creating a personal brand, knowing how to **design profitable menus, source ingredients wisely, and market your craft** is essential.

This chapter explores **the business side of mixology**, from cocktail pricing and menu engineering to branding and career development.

The Foundations of a Profitable Cocktail Program

A successful cocktail program isn't just about creativity—it must be **financially sustainable and operationally efficient**.

- **Drinks Should Be Profitable** – Every cocktail must balance quality with cost-effectiveness.
- **Menus Should Be Thoughtfully Designed** – Placement, descriptions, and pricing all influence what guests order.
- **Operations Must Be Efficient** – A well-structured bar keeps service smooth and consistent.

A well-run cocktail program creates a balance between creativity, efficiency, and profitability.

Menu Design: Crafting a Profitable & Engaging Cocktail Menu

A cocktail menu should be **visually appealing, easy to navigate, and strategically priced**.

1. The Psychology of Menu Placement

People's eyes naturally follow certain **patterns** when reading a menu. Placing **high-margin drinks in prime spots** can boost sales.

- **Top Right Corner** – The first place customers look (feature your signature cocktail here).
- **Middle Section** – A sweet spot where high-profit, balanced drinks should go.
- **Eye-Catching Names & Descriptions** – Drinks with intriguing names and well-crafted descriptions sell better.

Instead of listing ingredients generically, describe drinks with sensory appeal (e.g., "A smoky, citrus-forward twist on a classic Negroni with notes of burnt orange and rosemary").

2. Strategic Pricing & Cost Control

Cocktail pricing isn't random—it's a calculated balance of **ingredient costs, labor, and perceived value**.

The Standard Pricing Formula:

$$\text{MENU PRICE} = \frac{\text{COST OF INGREDIENTS}}{\text{DESIRED COST PERCENTAGE}}$$

Most bars aim for a **20–25% cost percentage**, meaning:

- » A cocktail that costs **$2.50 to make** should be priced at **$10-$12**.
- » Higher-end cocktails (with premium spirits or rare ingredients) can have a **lower cost percentage** but higher markup.

- **Keep Waste Low** – Every unused garnish, spilled drink, or poorly batched cocktail cuts into profit.
- **Use Cross-Utilization** – If you make a house-made syrup, ensure it's used in **multiple drinks** to maximize value.
- **Batch High-Volume Drinks** – Pre-batching Negronis or Espresso Martinis reduces service time and waste.

Test pricing by offering a limited-time special—if it sells well at a higher price, keep it there.

Sourcing Ingredients: Balancing Quality & Cost

The best cocktail programs source ingredients wisely, balancing **seasonality, sustainability, and profitability**.

- Choosing Spirits & Modifiers Wisely

- » **Stock Core Spirits for Versatility** – A great cocktail menu doesn't need **20 gins**—it needs a **well-chosen selection** of spirits that can work across multiple drinks.
- » **Consider Local & Craft Spirits** – Supporting local distilleries can create **unique menu offerings** and brand partnerships.

PRO TIP: If using an expensive ingredient, **pair it with lower-cost modifiers** to maintain profitability.

- Using Seasonal & Sustainable Ingredients
  - » **Buy Seasonal Fruits & Herbs** – They taste better and are more cost-effective.
  - » **Reduce Waste with Smart Ingredient Use** – Citrus peels can be used for syrups, coffee grounds for infusions, and leftover herbs for garnishes.
  - » **Make House-Made Ingredients When Possible** – Fresh syrups and infusions can be cheaper and higher quality than store-bought versions.

EXAMPLE: Instead of buying flavored syrups, make **rosemary honey syrup** by steeping fresh rosemary in honey and hot water.

Branding & Career Development for Mixologists

Your career as a mixologist doesn't have to stay behind the bar—**building a brand can open up new opportunities** in consulting, content creation, and product development.

1. Personal Branding:
Becoming an Authority in Mixology

- **Create a Signature Style** – Develop a recognizable approach to cocktails (e.g., herbal-forward, molecular, classic).
- **Use Social Media to Showcase Your Work** – Instagram, TikTok, and YouTube are powerful platforms for demonstrating cocktail techniques.
- **Engage with Industry Leaders** – Attend cocktail competitions, guest shifts, and networking events.

EXAMPLE: Bartenders like Ivy Mix (Leyenda, Brooklyn) and Ryan Chetiyawardana (Mr Lyan) built personal brands that led to bar ownership and product collaborations.

2. Expanding Beyond the Bar

Many mixologists expand their careers by moving into **education, consulting, and entrepreneurship**.

- **Cocktail Consulting** – Helping bars design menus and improve operations.
- **Teaching & Workshops** – Leading masterclasses for home bartenders or industry pros.
- **Product Development** – Creating signature bitters, syrups, or non-alcoholic spirits.
- **Writing & Content Creation** – Cocktail books, blogs, or online courses.

PRO TIP: Consider launching a **private cocktail service** for events—high-end clients pay premium rates for unique, curated drink experiences.

How to Stand Out in the Industry

In a competitive industry, here's how to **elevate yourself as a mixologist**:

- **Master Presentation & Storytelling** – People remember the experience, not just the drink.
- **Develop a Unique Selling Point** – Whether it's sustainability, experimental techniques, or a regional focus, specialize in something that sets you apart.
- **Stay Educated & Keep Innovating** – The best bartenders and mixologists never stop learning—from classic cocktail history to new mixology science.

Never stop tasting, testing, and refining your craft—great mixologists evolve with the industry.

Bringing It All Together

Mixology is more than just crafting cocktails—it's a fusion of **art, science, and storytelling**. Whether you're creating drinks for personal enjoyment, designing menus, or building a brand, the journey of a mixologist is one of **constant learning, experimentation, and evolution**. The techniques, principles, and insights in this book have given you the foundation to craft exceptional drinks, but the true magic comes from **your creativity, passion, and dedication to the craft**. Keep exploring, keep refining, and most importantly—keep making cocktails that inspire, surprise, and bring people together. **Your journey in mixology is just beginning.** Cheers!

Appendices

THIS SECTION SERVES AS YOUR quick-reference guide, featuring **essential flavor pairings, measurement conversions, glossary terms, and industry resources**. Whether you're developing new cocktails, adjusting recipes, or looking for further reading, this section will be your go-to resource.

APPENDIX A:

Essential Flavor Pairing Cheat Sheets

A well-crafted cocktail relies on balanced flavor pairings. Use these cheat sheets to inspire unique combinations.

Classic & Complementary Flavor Pairings

Primary Flavor	Complementary Pairings
Citrus (Lemon, Lime, Grapefruit, Orange)	Honey, thyme, vanilla, chili
Berries (Strawberry, Raspberry, Blackberry)	Basil, balsamic vinegar, cinnamon, black pepper
Tropical Fruits (Pineapple, Mango, Coconut)	Ginger, rum, nutmeg, mint
Stone Fruits (Peach, Cherry, Plum, Apricot)	Almond, vanilla, bourbon, rosemary
Spices (Cinnamon, Clove, Nutmeg, Star Anise)	Apple, honey, dark rum, brandy
Herbs (Basil, Mint, Rosemary, Thyme)	Citrus, cucumber, gin, vermouth
Bittersweet Ingredients (Campari, Aperol, Amaro, Coffee, Chocolate)	Orange, vanilla, smoky mezcal, cherry

Use this list when designing new cocktails or tweaking recipes to improve balance.

APPENDIX B:
Cocktail Measurement Conversions

Standard Liquid Measurements

Measurement	Equivalent
1 Dash	~⅛ Teaspoon
1 Teaspoon	5 mL
1 Tablespoon	15 mL
1 Ounce (oz)	30 mL
1 Jigger	1.5 oz (45 mL)
1 Cup	8 oz (240 mL)

Common Spirit Bottle Yields

Bottle Size	1.5 oz (Standard Pour)	2 oz (Double Pour)
750 mL (Standard Bottle)	~16-17 Cocktails	~12 Cocktails
1 Liter	~22 Cocktails	~16 Cocktails
1.75 L (Handle)	~39 Cocktails	~29 Cocktails

Use these conversions for scaling recipes or calculating inventory for events.

APPENDIX C:
Glossary of Mixology Terms

Basic Techniques

- **Shake** – Mixing ingredients vigorously with ice in a shaker.
- **Stir** – Gently mixing ingredients in a glass with ice for a smooth texture.
- **Muddle** – Pressing fresh ingredients (like herbs or fruit) to release flavors.
- **Dry Shake** – Shaking without ice, often used to aerate egg whites.

Common Ingredients

- **Simple Syrup** – Equal parts sugar and water, dissolved.
- **Shrub** – A vinegar-based syrup used for acidity.
- **Tincture** – A highly concentrated extract of an herb, spice, or fruit in alcohol.
- **Fat-Washing** – Infusing spirits with fats (butter, coconut oil, bacon) to add texture.

Glassware & Ice

- **Coupe Glass** – A short-stemmed glass used for elegant, stirred, or shaken drinks.
- **Rocks Glass** – A short glass used for spirit-forward cocktails over ice.
- **Collins Glass** – A tall, narrow glass ideal for highballs.
- **Clear Ice** – Large, slow-melting ice cubes with no air bubbles, made for slow dilution.

Refer to this glossary whenever you need to clarify cocktail terminology.

APPENDIX D:
Industry Resources & Further Reading

Must-Read Books for Mixologists

- *The Joy of Mixology* by Gary Regan – A deep dive into cocktail families.
- *Liquid Intelligence* by Dave Arnold – A scientific approach to cocktail techniques.
- *Death & Co: Modern Classic Cocktails* – An industry-standard guide from one of the top cocktail bars.
- *Meehan's Bartender Manual* by Jim Meehan – A comprehensive look at bar operations and cocktail philosophy.
- *Imbibe!* by David Wondrich – A historical perspective on cocktails and their origins.

Online Resources & Education

- **Tales of the Cocktail** (www.talesofthecocktail.org) – The premier cocktail festival and educational resource.
- **BarSmarts** (www.barsmarts.com) – Professional bartender training courses.
- **Difford's Guide** (www.diffordsguide.com) – An extensive cocktail recipe and ingredient database.
- **Cocktail Science** (www.seriouseats.com) – Explores the science behind great drinks.

Continued learning is key—keep reading, tasting, and experimenting to refine your craft.

APPENDIX E:

Classic Cocktail Ratios & Templates

These formulas serve as the foundation for countless cocktails. Use them as a **base for experimentation.**

1. The Sour Formula (Spirit + Citrus + Sweetener)

- Classic Example: **Whiskey Sour** (2 oz Whiskey, ¾ oz Lemon, ¾ oz Simple Syrup)
- Variation Idea: Swap whiskey for mezcal, lemon for grapefruit, and simple syrup for honey.

2. The Old Fashioned Formula (Spirit + Sugar + Bitters + Ice)

- Classic Example: **Old Fashioned** (2 oz Bourbon, ¼ oz Simple Syrup, 2 dashes Bitters)
- Variation Idea: Swap bourbon for aged rum, simple syrup for maple syrup, and bitters for chocolate bitters.

3. The Spritz Formula (Aperitif + Bubbles + Ice + Garnish)

- Classic Example: **Aperol Spritz** (2 oz Aperol, 3 oz Prosecco, 1 oz Soda Water)
- Variation Idea: Swap Aperol for elderflower liqueur, Prosecco for cider, and add thyme.

4. The Manhattan Formula (Spirit + Vermouth + Bitters)

- Classic Example: **Manhattan** (2 oz Rye, 1 oz Sweet Vermouth, 2 dashes Bitters)
- Variation Idea: Swap rye for cognac, bitters for amaro, and leave the sweet vermouth.

Once you understand these templates, you can create thousands of unique cocktails.

FINAL THOUGHTS:
The Never-Ending Journey of Mixology

Mixology is an **ever-evolving craft**—there is always more to learn, discover, and create. Whether you're perfecting a classic recipe, experimenting with cutting-edge techniques, or educating the next generation of bartenders, remember:

- A great cocktail is more than just a drink—it's an experience.
- Innovation comes from understanding the past while pushing boundaries.
- The best mixologists never stop learning.

Your journey in mixology is just beginning. Now, go shake, stir, and create something unforgettable.

About the Author

With over 15 years in the bar industry, Casey Linnell has dedicated his career to mastering and teaching the craft of mixology. As the founder of Casey's Cocktails, a mixology instruction business serving the greater Minneapolis, MN area, he has trained hundreds of individuals and bartenders in the art of cocktail creation, balance, and guest experience.

Passionate about elevating mixology beyond the bar, Casey wrote this book to show that anyone can become a great mixologist—without ever working a bar shift. He believes that mixology is more than just a profession; it's an art form that is constantly evolving. With new techniques, flavors, and styles emerging all the time, the creative possibilities are endless.

This is his second published book on mixology, continuing his mission to make the craft accessible, engaging, and deeply rewarding for professionals and enthusiasts alike.

A lifelong fan of tiki cocktails, Casey finds inspiration in their transportive flavors and intricate layers. His favorite cocktail? A Trader Vic Mai Tai, a drink that instantly conjures visions of sun-drenched beaches and tropical breezes.

Beyond mixology, Casey is a devoted husband, father of four, and a follower of Jesus Christ. He attributes everything in his life—his family, his work, and his passion for the craft—to the grace and love of Christ.

When he's not teaching, experimenting with new flavors, or writing about cocktails, you'll find him spending time with his wife and children, cherishing the blessings of family and faith.

www.ingramcontent.com/pod-product-compliance
Lightning Source LLC
Chambersburg PA
CBHW050916160426
43194CB00011B/2424